CONVERSATIONS WITH MYSELF
Poems Stories Reflections

MARK SHOENFIELD

ISBN-13: 978-1547276684

For Frances, my partner in life, and my moral compass who always points due North.

Contents

Poems

Stories

Haiku's

Poems

Friendship

The thread of friendship
often weaves itself around
different people who are quite similar

Sometimes the threads become frayed
in need of an emotional tailor
And like an old suit, some can be let in or let out
Some are retained forever in plastic
in the rear of the closet
And some are dispatched to Good Will

Remoteness

Should I be troubled by your remoteness?
Am I the cause, the catalyst or just the observer?
Do I leave you space to navigate through your fog?
Hand you a raincoat or compass?
Or do I elicit your prompt attention,
shine a light in your face or gently tug at your sleeve?
Send me a sign.
Which way does the breeze blow?
Can even you discern the swirl?

Certainty

You can be sure that it will end. It always does
Be it the calm serenity of well crafted life rhythms
Or the sloppy seas of emotional white caps
Life's rhythms like electricity pulse in a path that
flows beyond beginning, middle and end
We think we see the path, the sign posts and buoys
But like an underground river the water seeks the path
of least resistance
And our lives take invisible unfathomable twists and
turns below the surface
We think we are the captain; we need to think we are
in charge
But suppose we only control the rudder in an endless
sea
We cannot control the wind and tide, we steer as best
we can
Not as in control as we like to think
That is our nature

Creation

The thrill of tapping that creative energy
Watching the creation start from nothing,
sure of its purity
Being a conduit, a seer, channeling that
unconscious stream to the surface
and watching it mix with oxygen and sunlight
The pure form constituting substance,
standing alone and upright
Unique and new to the world
Is that not joy?
How sweet the poet

Ode to Manhattan in December

Leaving Madison Square Garden,
tickets in hand on a cold December evening
A future date secured with 20,000 others
to see an event
Stutter stepping up 7th Ave.
dodging frenetic rush hour pedestrians
Like two armies trapped in a pinball machine
careening here and there, on my way to the Port
Authority terminal, that sling shot to New Jersey
The hustle and bustle feeds your brain a super
charged diet leading to a New York high
Your thoughts stimulated by the rushing masses
and ricocheting multi colored lights
A plethora of sights and sounds, your portals
are wide open to receive the direct feed
You are a player as well as the audience
on this island stage of a play

Turn onto the wide vista of 34th street
vendors with foreign accents selling roasted
chestnuts, their aroma mingling with the excited
conversations of the holiday masses
Walking out paces the cars and buses mired
in seasonal molasses
Humanity streams by, winners and losers
like jelly beans side by side in the largest jar in
America
all navigating their different journeys
All these lives swarming like bees in a frenzy
and Manhattan being the largest holy honey-
comb in existence

the thrill to participate, each individual magnifies the
mix, adds some voltage
No responsibilities hang over your head,
the night is cold and clear, no entanglements
Free and open to absorb the cosmic life force
in all its strange and subtle ways
is this the umbilical cord that the beat poets
spoke of?
Beat to hippie to rock to rap,
to all the same oneness
Cluing into the connection of the no fault
collision of your life with the universe?
Perhaps, but you gotta scrape your own knee
and singe your nostrils with wasabi
You can't read about it, you must allow
yourself to give birth to your own experience

I have my tickets, I have Manhattan,
Manhattan has me
let the symbiotic journey continue!

Stairway

Sometimes you get a glimmer of the past and future at
the same time
As I exited a train in Brooklyn and proceeded
along the platform heading for the stairs
before me stood my past and future at the same time
The link between these two being only my
consciousness

The stairway, wide enough for six
had dual handrails
The older outside rail was wooden with
chipped yellow paint
the newer inner rail, was metal, smooth and
shiny requiring little or no maintenance
The departing passengers were funneled up an
inverted Y to the street

there was a slim young man wearing a grey
sweatshirt, tight blue jeans and white sneakers
he bounded up the middle of the stairs with near
effortlessness
He was not aware of the speed and grace at which he
proceeded
There was balance, deftness and silent fluidity
as he covered the two flights of steps
in but a thoughtless youthful moment

To my right was a gentleman of undetermined
older age
He used a cane to aid him on his slow ascent
up these same stairs
what hair remained was white, patched and thin

He was over dressed for the day and reached for
the older wooden rail for support
He lifted each foot in a careful manner to be
sure it cleared the next step

In a moment the youthful man was gone from view,
like my own youthfulness
Though the older man would still be on the stairs after
I had passed him,
he was still in my future

How interesting the mind, to create order
from the random bits of reality
we are all story tellers to ourselves,
free to devise our own insights
because there is always a stairway
leading somewhere

Kidney Stone Part 1

Out of the blue
the worst night of your life
pain to bring you to your knees
pain to disassemble your wired brain
pain to let you know whose boss
pain you will not forget
torture with no conscience
the body traitor
emergency room
IV's, drugs, time
the stone is gone
the crisis fades
the memory scar imbedded forever

Pain- Kidney Stone Part 2

A dark marauder that silently traitorizes
your body
there is no thought, conscious intent on its part
spasmodic contractions following their design
simple stimulus responses that renders you in horror
at your lack of alternatives
no exit is written on the door
you cannot remain you cannot leave
beyond panic into that next ethereal realm
how to survive its clutches, that becomes the
question?
no deals can be struck
you are the passenger until the ride is over

A Kiss

I offer you a kiss
hidden inside a small leather pouch
that is tightly tied by a leather draw string
bewildered eyes communicate that
your nimble fingers do not know how to open the
pouch
my kiss will remain invisible
because it was meant for no other

Father and Son

On a warm June evening in my 54th year
my 16 year old son asks me to hit him fungos
my diminished prowess clearly states
who is the coach and who is the player
I hit rainbow fly balls to his left and right
he sprints lithely, with grace, speed and
determination after the cowhide spheres
arcing to earth
sweat glistens on his brow and mine
I see the present and past collide in
intergenerational confusion
vicariously reliving the simple uncluttered
pleasure of pure pursuit
to test one's physical limits against time and space
I loft one hope and challenge after another
into the twilight
and my son gives his all in the chase
he is not consciously aware of the metaphors
of this exchange
my inner delight is immense in this physical
give and take
the baseball tossed from my hand to bat to sky
to be snared in his glove and thrown back to me
the pattern repeated over and over
caught up in this rhythmic dance,
wishing time would pause in this magic moment
of ordinariness
I humbly acknowledge that life doesn't get any
sweeter than this

It's OK

I was 22 when my father died in 1973
I have outlived my father by 3 years already
we never spoke as equals
I fear I will leave my son long before he reaches 22
what can I tell him now?
how not to raise his anxieties?
how not to buttress his mistrust of the universe?
how to tell him it's alright, he'll get through
he'll be fine?
the seedling has been nurtured and will grow towards
the sun
it no longer needs the stake for support
we have not yet spoken as equals,
a dream I hold close to my heart
but I can tell him that I love him
and I always will be with him
and he with me, this I can be sure of
as sure as I see my father's face in the mirror
will he find this comforting if we never speak as
equals?
I trust in time he will

Inside Out Outside In

We all carry on an inside conversation in our mind
What we really think as we make our way through the
world
These thoughts are our biased observations culled
from experience and expectations
The outside world exists with no knowledge
or care of our inner thoughts
We rarely show our inner dialogue the light of day
We are wise enough to guard these thoughts for fear
of being wrong or foolish
what if we could react to only what is, and shut down
this mind, remove the ego and judgments,
can we see the world for what it is,
quiet the mind and shelve the distortions?
Focus on the external here and now

To leave the coffee shop, breakfast in hand, pass the
people in the lobby on my way to the elevator,
ride up and walk to my desk without a single internal
thought
These are muscles I will exercise in order to let the
outside in and keep the inside out

View from Atop

I'm standing on top of the mountain
the air is sweet and the view expansive
I never thought I'd get here
I can finally exhale and feel exalted
Most of the impediments were self imposed
I wasn't really fighting the mountain but myself
It is with this knowledge I know
no other mountain will be quite as tall

Maturity

Where is the joy
Where is the bliss?
It's always right behind the cloud
in fact it may be the cloud itself
Do not think me simplistic
I have tasted the ashes and they are not sweet

Scary

I am a curious person I like to know things

When you are in a long term relationship
and you want more from the other person
who is not giving it
I wonder if that person is capable of giving more?
Would they have arrived at the same place with
someone else?
Are our personality's level seeking like water?
Over time do we bottom out, only to spike when
pricked by some event?
Scary

I'd like to know why we finally understand something
after being told it many, many times before?
What is it about the last time that makes it settle in,
why were we deaf before?
What clicks on an emotional level to make absorption
possible?
It makes you wonder what else you've been missing,
failing to hear?
Scary

I'd like to know why we resist what is good for us and
cannot overcome the change, the pain, the fear, for
our greater good?
Why do we work against our better interests?
Scary
Of course these are not easy questions
and we have some mighty strong investments
in holding to our status quo

Gratefully I have found that the fear of not changing
has propelled me to sometimes act
The scary thought of just staying in one place
not changing, can motivate, to parachute
into that great beyond
that is always different than what I imagined
Almost always for the greater good,
yet I stay on my heels and not my toes
when the bomb bay door opens wide
and rarified yonder gently beckons

The Topper

I was sitting on my Brooklyn front stoop some 35
years ago
with mescaline and speed joyously traversing through
my synapses, producing a super high definition of
intricate delights for the mind and senses

much to my surprise my mother's car matter of factly
pulled up into its customary place out front
Even with the speed at work, I needed to think
quickly
How to be, how to act, what to say?
I first traveled the path of denial, acting as if
everything was "normal"
"Hi Ma, nothing, your home early"
But the drug induced euphoria made me shoot the
moon for honesty, as I needed to share the moment as
my happiness was busting out
I confessed my situation and persuaded my mother to
accompany me for a walk in the park

I rambled on voicing the crystal clear cosmic truths so
plain to see
with the mescaline pulling back the curtain to reveal
the universe's simple truths
I wanted my mother to listen, to share the moment, to
let me try and explain what I was experiencing, to
give me the floor and let me run

she couldn't

she had to turn the moment around making herself the
center

she had to top my experience and steal my spotlight
I don't think I expressed my hurt and disappointment
but it was much worse than coming down
from the drug that day

and less pain and more disappointment
linger 35 years later
how to fight the infantile rage to get others to change
and learn to accept what is
that is a struggle of mass proportion

Aging

At the barber shop the other day in Montclair
the barber held up a mirror to demonstrate his skill
I clearly saw an emerging bald spot for the first time,
on what appeared to be **my** head
I have age spots springing up who knows where
and lines on my face grow increasingly deeper

Why am I surprised?
Why do we think this aging thing happens only to
others?
Who can we discuss this panic with?
People seem resigned
they sigh and say "whatta ya' going to do,
it could be worse"
But I want **to do** something
my ego is offended
where did this ego come from?
Is this external changing but a visual clue for my dim-
witted mind that we are evolving and no amount of
work, play or money can evade or stop this life cycle?

How to embrace physical decline?
Can that be taught?
We observe every single erosion with increasing
anxiety
Can we enjoy the decline without the clichés?
How not to compare ourselves with, what we were, to
what we are
How not to compare ourselves with others of our own
age?

How to just be?

Outsider

I am an outsider
I know this role well
I do not join, I observe
I understand the gains and losses well
I am untethered, protected, nimble and free
I am the captain of a ship of one
I make many false untested assumptions
I fear and crave connections I decide not to make
To lose my aloneness (would falsely) I think create a
debt I could never repay
I value safety over connectedness, as if the two are at
odds
In time I will know this is false
I hold all the power of my own dismay
I am stronger than I let myself know
To give up the familiar for the just out of reach
I must extend my arm, knowing there is so much to
gain!
To test the waters of relaxing my own constraints
I must wade into the shallow pool and find my
footing
I must trust my soul to swim, the body is buoyant
My toes a lift off the bottom my heart is thrilled
I will stay here and enjoy until I am ready to venture
further

A September Day in Cape May NJ

On the beach in Cape May, New Jersey
my teenage son and I begin a baseball
catch in the early evening
We are way back from the water, where the sand still
retains the day's warmth
and other beach goers have long since departed
Gulls peck at the sand looking for morsels as the surf
gently breaks in its rhythmic pattern
My wife sits and watches us from a distance,
forming the unbalanced triangle that is our life

We increase the distance between our long tosses
My leather glove snaps a sharp crack as it embraces
the hurling sphere
I return a well rehearsed overhand throw that has
many years of practice behind it
Our long shadows lengthen as the sun slowly sets and
we increase our pace, throwing with greater velocity
and heightened focus
A white three masted schooner skirts the horizon
A kite ripples in the increasing breezes high above
my son's head
The tethered string being held by a far away girl
Puffs of white sand arise around the ankles of my son
on every toss
His skinny, well tanned body and freckled nose are
absorbed in the moment
Low throws hug the sand and kick up grains
that stings my shins
An older departing couple apologizes for interrupting
us as they pass between my son and me, lugging their

beach chairs, floral towels and a large white canvas
bag
I silently thank them for the opportunity to rest my
now tiring arm
A slight chill in the salty air denotes a change
the summer is ending,
as is my middle age as well as my son's innocence
Ready or not, we all have a new season to embrace

Push & Pull

You say we are not connected
You turn your face away when you enter the door
You speak not a word in my direction
as if this is fine
You exclude me and yet seek my closeness
Check your own actions before you call me remote
Do I care if you are replaying another's role learned a
long time ago?
Or even if you are improvising on the fly
Just do not ask for my kiss when you turn away
I can love you but not be your savior

Is It Real?

How to distinguish the sincerity of social
or business interactions?
This is something that I have never been good at
"You're looking well. I like your tie, you're very
astute"

Yes politeness is the grease that smoothes the social
contract
Does it matter if it's sincere, as long as it moves the
train of friendship or the deal down the tracks?
I am easily seduced by the facade,
wanting to believe the hollow praise
without weighing from whence it comes
Time alas has taught me to chew before swallowing
but how do we evaluate the flatter's gifts?
If the confirm what we already know,
if the speaker is someone we value?
Time may or may not resolve the issue
The best scam is one the mark never learns about
Alas the paranoids never get to rest

Where Do I Fit In?

I am a man, a husband a father
Where do I fit in
I am a son a brother a writer
Where do I fit in
I am a citizen an American a New Jerseyite
Where do I fit in
I am a traveler a worker a lover
Where do I fit in
I am a consumer a baker a creator
Where do I fit in
I am a friend a fan a traveler
Where do I fit in
I am a union member a TV viewer a money spender
Where do I fit in
I am a sleeper an eater a car keeper
Where do I fit in
I am a human a commuter a kitchen floor sweeper
Where do I fit in
I am a crier a buyer a man stuck in mire
Where do I fit in,   where do I fit in
                    Where do I fit in?

Does Size Matter?

Four dimes, two nickels and a penny
in the sandy pocket of a man standing on a beach in
Long Island
which is an area in North America
which is part of a country called the United States
which is a continent on the planet earth
which is part of the Milky Way
which is one galaxy of millions
which is like a grain of sand at the beach

We know we are but an atom in the universe
Yet the man frets he won't be able to buy a newspaper
to read about the baseball game played last night

I Have Met Madness

I have met madness
the implosion of the self
invisible waves of doom and dread
battering the sense of self

Knowing reality is receding
on its own accord, wondering
how to grip the sand as
the ocean pulls you out down deep
where no light serves as a beacon of hope

I used to wonder, how, lacking a tangible event
one could take one's own life?
I wonder no more, a door was ajar
that let me peak into the blackness
that sliver of angst and despair
so dark as to rob the soul and reason
at the same time
The kicker is that you know it's not real or valid
and yet your thoughts orbit over and around
themselves in non ending elliptical brain knots
bouncing off stone like cliffs

The terrible truth that your mind can turn on itself and
break the man
exponentially expands the vulnerability of this world
The threat of violence whether intentional or not can
now be known to come from both the exterior and
interior realm
The physical self, sabotaged, so inconceivable to
others, yet so real to the victim

is a humbling experience never to be fully expunged
from the residual psyche
The simple truths, laws of nature, guidelines to sanity
so taken for granted
have revealed themselves to be but a thin porous
foundation
Oh to return to just the oh, oh sweet sense of every
day boredom
would be like the ecstasy of an LSD trip

Corridors

A beautiful exotic young woman walking down the
corridor talking to her two male superiors
Both older married men are very attracted to her
voluptuous body
the straight black hair, abundant breasts and well
proportioned features stir a primal
attraction that is obvious, yet goes unspoken
none of the three acknowledges other than
the shop talk at hand
nothing will happen today, tomorrow or any other day
Yet one man tries his best to show how nice he is,
how supportive, informative, amusing and kind he
can be
The other man does not try at all, he is curt,
straight forward with decidedly no sense of humor
Each man has chosen to view middle age from a
different corridor

A Smile

My wife has decided to take up golf at age 53
This is not an easy thing to do
And so she visits the driving range, clubs in hand to
practice her swing and try to become
more proficient
She works hard harnessing her strength in a
concentrated manner
I sit and watch, offering gentle suggestions
Some miss hits produce weak grounders
or anemic slices

What makes it all worthwhile is when she smacks the
dimpled white ball squarely
and it rises skyward supplanting her previous best
A huge smile that starts in her sole and radiates
outward, brighter with more color than any bouquet,
blooms upon her face
She is as thrilled with the shot,
as I am to see that smile

Rehearsing

Out of the blue my son asks to go to the batting cages
His interest in this pursuit always surprises me
To face a mechanical arm hurling baseballs in your
direction
in which you pay a fee, seems rather strange
He politely waits his turn, as other testosteroned
teens channel their aggression trying to mash rubber
baseballs into screen netting
You compete against the machine, against yourself
and against former and future "contestants"
all with the world's invisible eyes upon you
It's a male teenage rite of passage, carnival sledge
hammer, ring the bell competition
There are no girls here to impress, this competition is
mano a mano
This self test my son thinks is about muscle strength
and hand eye coordination
I view it as an adolescent self confidence test, prior to
the pursuit of female companionship
Mastery of one set of skills to the pursuit of larger
goals
I happily deposit the tokens in the metal box and
watch my son take his swings

October 10, 2005 NY Yankees Lose ($208 million)

There are certain days of the year to celebrate
Christmas your birthday and New Years
But few are sweeter to toast, by raising a glass of
booze
than when the pinstriped NY Yankees lose!
High priced arrogant and smug
No Yankee was smiling when the final out was in the
pitcher's glove
All baseball fans know, what the Yankees must now
hear,
eliminated again, wait until next year
all baseball fans have been down this road before
And now the Yankees have been shown the door
Weep not for them, their lack of a ring
because of their motto "cash is king"
Some championships you cannot buy
but this is something the Yanks will always try

Love

To lick that first drop of nectar from your flesh
none others to ever taste exactly the same
only journeys to try and recapture that experience
that is our special gift to each other
a life time of firsts

Emotional Photographs

Do not be scared
Remember these are but emotional photographs
Each one distinct and separate
An isolated moment in time
Yes they are woven together
Like the patchwork quilt that covers our bed
And we choose carefully which ones to reveal to
ourselves and to others
Hunt through the shoebox of my mind
until you find one that pleases you
I trust your gentle hand and heart to find my truest
image of you
For you have given me the film to reflect back your
true loving image

4 a.m. Demons

It's all how you look at it
My point of view, your point of view,
the world's point of view
Waking at 4 a.m. from deep slumber,
all I see and feel is my warped distorted view
I have no self confidence at 4 a.m.
I'm a snarled mass of panic, indecision and dread
Obsessionally fighting invisible demons that don't
even consider me a real contender
yet they seem to have nothing better to do with their
time than turn my psyche into a car wreck
At 7 a.m. they will be gone, time zones away
tormenting someone else I guess
But I need a 4 a.m. strategy to bridge me over
to dawn,
that reality of a life preserver that bobs you up out of
the reach of the demons grasp
That morning light, a beacon to sanity
so that you can deal with what is,
rather than those inner dark tides, taking reason and
judgment under, to strafe and cut them on
the shells of Neptune's belly
Pounding heart, adrenaline surging, all springing forth
from where?
The unconscious, biology gone amiss or some
misaligned learning process?
Chose your source, all as real and valid as a
nightmare
I do not care!
Return me to that deep sweet protected anesthetic that
is a respite from the chaos

Closet Mind

Hey we all have clothes closets
that Rorschach test, that class indicator of who we are
Our seasonal skins hung on hangers;
mine sorted by color
Do my 100% cottons indicate I'm pure?
Do my plethora of plain blue grey and white shirts
indicate my blandness?
Do my greens, hunter, forest and aqua indicate my
trendy hipness?
Let's not forget my earth tones to show I prefer to
blend with nature
There's an old Nehru jacket that I can't bring myself
to discard,
you fill in the blank what that indicates
It's hard to be profound or emotionally moving when
discussing one's closet
But isn't "closet" a metaphor of something we keep
hidden?
And don't our clothes show us off, go figure
just remember, clothes make the man or so the
capitalists and psychiatrist's would have us believe
and didn't all the radicals of the 1960's
wear a similar uniform?
So remember, thread lightly when you lapel hole me
as an off the rack kind of guy
and I'll review you as a book superficially clad in
but one jacket
from an assortment of many more in your
publisher's closet

Happy Birthday Frances

We celebrate the day of your birth
for when you entered this world you added to its
mirth
Innocent and pure, honest and true
were all glad to have gotten the opportunity
to know you
A day to reflect and look back over the past
we hope you agree, it's been quite a blast
With much more to come,
we all hope to contribute
to making it fun

Happy Birthday

The Good Old Days (October 2005)

Late October, Montclair, NJ, Tuesday 10 p.m.
It's raining outside
The house is warm and dry, we are healthy and fed
I'm in the kitchen, a Dylan CD playing while I sip red
wine and stuff artichokes for tomorrows
evening meal
I've been to work, made dinner, shuttled my son here
and there and purchased future provisions
from the A&P
My wife is in the bedroom watching TV as she
relaxes from a long hard day of work and commuting
My son watches a different show in the living room
after a day of high school, homework, track practice
and an evening art class
We are all in our cocoons, taking a respite from the
day's responsibilities,
the day's news and mundane conversations have been
played out

In the future no one will remember this day
it will fade and blur like most of those behind us
We are a family in transition, like all families
(without knowing it) and this is but one snapshot in
time
it's been a busy uneventful day, I'll gladly take
I'll try and remember this day
It's our Thornton Wilder's "Our Town" kind of day
Soon we will queue up for showers brush our teeth
and prepare for tomorrow

How much we take for granted

Separation

Baseball was my life as a youth
It served me well, it gave me focus, identity, notoriety
it protected me from loneliness, isolation and
questioning
My success spurred me on to a greater love of the
sport
Its tentacles still tether me to a larger world today
To lose one's young self in the physical dedication of
a game was something special
My two brothers, one older one younger chose
different sports to compete in
They needed their own identity and instinctively
another road so as not to trespass
I have tried to pass my passion to my son
He does not see it as a gift I revere
He does not understand my motivation
yet feels the strong gravitational pull of trying to
please a father
Like my brothers he has chosen another sport to
compete in and though dedicated and committed, he
does not have the fire

His skill and talent lie in the world of art,
an area that I and my wife are quite ignorant of
But I see the same commitment, passion and
dedication that I held for baseball take root in his
developing identity
And when you roll the dice of parenthood there's no
telling what numbers come up
But what a special pleasure in watching skill and
passion merge in your young child

Cognizant that he needs his own identity, perhaps it's a blessing that his talent lies in an area so foreign to my wife and me

This distance dilutes our urge to tamper and let's him follow his own path, which he must ultimately do anyway

My wife and I stand back and admire the creation we have supplied the raw materials for

and watch with expectant curiosity whatever new art will be produced for in our loving eyes there are no miss strokes

Brooklyn Is in My Soul

I have not lived in Brooklyn for many many years,
but Brooklyn is in my soul
I can tell you my street in Brooklyn was not fully
paved in 1960
I can tell you of Irish and Italian boys kicking schools
books out of my hands for fun
I can tell you of July 4th fireworks and Roman
candles that sounded like a "shock and awe" invasion
and left the streets smelling of gun powder the
following day
I can tell you of finding used prophylactics in the
sand at the beach
I can tell you of social and ethnic ghettos defined by
invisible borders
I can tell you that our neighbor Mrs. Catto, whose
husband use to beat her, made the best apple pies
from the tart green apples that grew in her yard
I can tell you of my family before divorce, before
heart attacks and before Viet Nam

O, Brooklyn is in my soul
Sawdust on butcher shop floors, when I wasn't tall
enough to see over counters
School yard punch ball, tight black chinos, pizzerias
with soccer broadcasts in Italian
Orange neon signs glowing in Hebrew lettering in the
Jewish delis
Orthodox Jews strolling down Ocean Parkway
Elevated trains, with straw woven seats and broken
windows that took us to "the city"
through neighborhoods as different as European cities

O, Brooklyn is in my soul
Working class families living "the dream" in what
seemed like hundreds of identical six- story high
apartment houses
Middle class families in private homes on twenty by
one hundred foot plots with tiny back yards
I remember playing in vacant lots we called "the
jungle" now replaced by concrete and commerce
I remember graffiti, dirty streets and petty crimes,
imbedded within the landscape
Always an edge of something in the Brooklyn night
I could tell you of neighborhoods to avoid, juvenile
delinquents and petty thugs;
rocks in socks on Halloween, a weapon to separate
you from your Waldbaum's bag of candy
fast talking dim witted street savvy characters always
with personal agenda
juxtaposed by polite law abiding accented immigrants
who wore Yankee ball caps and had many children

O, Brooklyn is in my soul
Katie's, a hole in the wall grocery store at the end of a
residential block, with two cent pretzels and
individual licorice sticks in covered tall glass jars

Neighbors who sat on stoops and talked on warm
sultry nights
Fresh hot bagels, Sheepshead Bay, the Avalon and
Graham movie theaters, PS 194, James Madison High
School

I can tell you, I do not wax nostalgic for the 4th
largest city in America

I long for the ill perceived connections of my early
life
We are all shackled to our past, we long for what is
missing and what we think we had
My family was intact then, friends and relatives were
within a familiar gravitational pull
Now, none of my "family" reside in Brooklyn, dead,
scattered, weightless in homogenized America
I am lost, I am lonely

We try to reinvent ourselves in the genetic husk from
our past
But no matter what my age or location, a certain
sense of Brooklyn lives on in me
Lessons and perceptions ingrained there have a
defining lasting quality

I cannot return to Brooklyn
My Brooklyn no longer exists
there are only strangers in my homeland now
And all that is left for me are my distorted memories,
and a permanent sense of unmooring,
And the undeniable fact that Brooklyn is in my soul

My Father

My father loved French cheese, good scotch
and women who weren't my mother
My father didn't clean up messes like fighting with
my brothers
It's been over 45 years since his death
and I forgive or miss him like no other

Thoughts- Mark David Chapman

I read about Mark David Chapman the other day
You know, the guy who assassinated John Lennon all
those years ago
Chapman said he was a loser and killing Lennon
made him a somebody
Maybe Chapman should have watched Marlon
Brando in "On The Waterfront" instead
Maybe he would have aspired to something different,
better
Maybe he should have stayed in his head, like the rest
of us
I have treaded lightly on this earth, and that's fine
with me

The other day I was sitting on the train when a tall
beautiful young black woman sat down across from
me
she seemed to stare or hold her gaze on me a little too
long
so I returned her fix

She was long boned and seemed a little
uncomfortable with her height
As if finding it difficult to find her grace in this world
I'm sure her slight awkwardness was an unconscious
shield that acted like reverse camouflage to men
I always look at the corner of a woman's eye to
determine her age
When you focus there you also cannot help to see the
entire face
The woman was young but not that young

You can tell by the way her black eyes settled on me,
she was looking for some answer to her internal
question, or was it a statement?
That's not for me to know
She had clear unblemished skin, perfect features with
hair tightly drawn straight back and tied with a
colored band
Her small delicate ears held tiny diamond earrings
that neither distracted nor called attention but rather
blended in subtlety to enhance her in an understated
way

Being much older I valued her beauty more so than
perhaps a younger man
Age bringing a wisdom and appreciation not yet
acquired by the young
What if I used my guile, older sophistication and
wealth to impress this beautiful young innocent
nubile?
What if I was somehow able to impregnate her, and
our children would be beautiful long limbed
mulattoes?
How strange a life turn would that be?
Suppose instead of treading lightly,
I decided to jump on the trampoline of life to see just
how high I could bound?
And what if I impregnated every woman I possibly
could just for the heck of it?
To turn my life upside down and run amok without a
shred of morality or decency, max out those credit
cards, really live for the moment, let someone else
clean up the mess!

The train came to a halt, two stations past my stop,

the beautiful young woman was nowhere to be seen
In her seat, now sat a heavy set construction worker,
forty something, with white plaster dust on his face
and wearing a sweat stained grey sweat shirt
He was not looking at me when my life channel reset

Why couldn't Mark David Chapman stay in his head
like the rest of us,
with his thoughts taking absurd wild leaps off very
high cliffs
and why couldn't he miss the train stop near the
Dakota building that John Lennon lived in?

Duality

Basically there are two worlds out there,
both are real or so I think
Last night I watched television
This morning I listened to the radio
and read the paper
I and my friends, acquaintances, in fact everyone I
know live our lives in quiet unspectacular ways
I guess we are lucky, it seems real
Yet all the stories and news and entertainment
that I see reflect an alien world that I also believe to
be real
Our heads are full of this duality and yet we
comfortably accept these parallel worlds
One is OUR world the one we inhabit on a daily basis
the other is the world we see, hear and read about so
it's mostly in our mind
We are really quite trusting when you think about it

Clouds 11/05

On a warm July day when I was 12 years old
I lay on my back on the grass in the center of Marine
Park smelling the decomposing grass
that had been cut the day before

In such a large open field glancing towards the
horizon I felt the curvature of the earth in the crease
where the earth and sky meet
Feeling the pull of gravity on my body and a slight
dizziness I stared upward and watched the clouds
spread across the sky constantly
forming and reforming into new shapes in their
perpetual path eastward
The winds of the upper atmosphere pushing the
reluctant clouds that defiantly obeyed but not without
some resistance
They were swept along unable to pause
and constantly morphed into something new

When you concentrated on the clouds you noticed
how quickly they moved
Most people don't give it much thought,
they don't have time to watch clouds
They live their lives and rarely notice,
but for a casual glance skyward
forming a mental shorthand of how the weather will
affect them

Although the park was fairly crowded, children's
shouts and ballgame chatter were distant and muffled
on the flat open plain

I remember that day even though it was over 40 years
ago, what happened to those clouds,
what happened to that 12 year old boy?
We each swiftly moved across the horizon,
forming and reforming
The changes both slow and swift at the same time
I like watching clouds they remind me to pause
and remember there are no pauses
And I too follow the winds of time,
but like the clouds not without some
resistance

Driving Alone Late at Night

Riding home in the car way past midnight gives one
time to reflect
The radio, playing low smoky bluesy sad love songs
quietly filling the car with a melancholy
atmosphere
The endless monotony and the late hour helps
construe thoughts of loss and wondering what ifs
Reliving old memories of girlfriends and lovers
wondering how often I surface in their long road trips,
as they appear before me now
Long ago memories have frozen end points like
icicles but that is not their true end
they are in fact walking breathing people we loved,
like watching an old movie over and over
while knowing the actors are presently shooting an
ongoing sequel that you will never get to see
Memories like exit signs approach appear and recede,
again and again

I harbor no ill will to any of my these formers
We are all each other's emotional connectors,
puzzles and grist for long late night car rides
home ... ... hopefully to a new lover

A Wish

My wife never saw her parents hold hands or kiss
with passion
She has four siblings so something went on in her
house
My son does not see real affection between my wife
and me
And he, like my wife did, will grow up thinking this
is some kind of norm

While inwardly growing a sadness that I cannot
explain away with words
I hope that he will be wise enough to veer to the
opposite
and make grand lavish shows of affection to his wife
in front of all
not as a role model or actor but because he cannot
contain himself in the pleasure he feels
in giving of himself
and not be constrained by the visions
of his youth

Operating Room

You lie on a gurney in the operating room
Shivering, lying on your side, as you wait
White blanket draped over you
IV in your arm, drip, drip, drip
Is it fear or hope swirling through the saline drip that
enters through a steel needle taped to a constrained
blue vein?
You're asked your date of birth
The bright lights help others to see
Fear has given way to docile acceptance
You listen to your electronic heart beat,
beep, beep, beep
You're asked your date of birth again
Busy people scamper about as you lie motionless
You look up and see a syringe, plunger up, connected
to the clear plastic tubing
You're asked your date of birth again
Your body has surrendered, it is theirs
You know when you awaken there will be small
strange cuts, bruises and news
mysterious violations in which the mind is sheltered
but the body offended
Your mind searches for rational escape hatches
This is your test of faith or acceptance
You're asked your date of bir...............

White Pages and Time

The challenge of the white page
To muster something from within of value or wit
To troll with a bucket in the stream of your
unconscious and pour forth something new to this
world, never before seen or spoken aloud
How to initiate a written creation?

More than time and imagination
a combustible spark in the synapse is needed
to kindle an idea from a spark to a raging forest fire
And then to catch the attention of all those who smell
smoke on the breeze, who then get on the phone and
alert the authorities
Extra, extra, extra call the press and public radio
this creative idea is out of control

Before you know it they'll make it a play
and translate it into multiple languages
then a movie with the stars of the day
It will be taught in all the finest universities
for generations to come

And eventually, over time, over generations, it will be
forgotten, buried as if it had never existed
For nothing, nothing outlives the passage of time
And everything is displaced by the present
And others will sit before a new white page

It's All How You Look at It

It's all how you look at it, that's what I think
My wife's too hot I'm too cold
Were both sure the others wrong
Doesn't matter what the thermometer says

I give my son his allowance
He thinks it's too little, I think it's too much
It's all how you look at it

I think my wife is too neat, she thinks I'm too messy
It's all how you look at it

So what are you going to do when your each sure
you're right?
How to address the conflict, well
It's all how you look at it
Concede, eat shit, dig in, rant and rave, ignore
steam roll, accept, agree compromise, change?
It's all how you look at it

Comes with the Territory

One New Year's Eve my wife and I went to see an old
folk singer
Several days later I sat in a leather recliner reading
the NY Times and listened to a CD of the same artist,
he now being 65 years old
35 years prior my father sat in a leather recliner
listening to his new stereo and expensive speakers
listening to the same artist in his prime
I, then 17 years old lounged on the sofa hearing the
recording over and over
So listening to this artist in the present
warmly, fondly, nostalgically took me back 35 years
when my father was alive and was 45 years old

My 16 year old son happened to wander through the
living room
and I wanted to share the moment and continue
the link from father to son, I asked him to stop and
listen for awhile
I hoped some magical effect would occur
and he would somehow be delighted in completing
some invisible circle
He listened for a moment before declaring
that one of his favorite TV shows was starting
and he rapidly left the room
If every parent had a quarter for each time their child
broke their heart by not loving or appreciating
something as much as they did
then the golden retirement would surely have very
wealthy sunsets

Artist Richie Havens- Album Mixed Bag
Fisher stereo receiver AR2 speakers
Coyle Street Brooklyn Theodore Shoenfield
Riverview Drive Montclair NJ Mark Shoenfield
TV show The Sopranos Sam Shoenfield

At the Open Poetry Reading

At the open poetry reading I confess,

I was born in Paterson, New Jersey
I don't like Alan Ginsberg
I'm uncomfortable with his homosexual references
I don't like John Updike
he frustrates me, I want him to get on with
the plot
Enough with the flowery description

I don't like the obscure incoherent poems
in the New Yorker
How can a poem be good if it's so high brow
most folks are left clueless after two readings?

I don't like Yeats, Shelly, Pound or William Carlos
Williams
I can't relate

And maybe this promotes one to write
thinking their voice is unique
And full of conceit, self righteously
plowing forward with a voice that is true to ones
self

Hoping to be the brightest peacock in the yard
arrogantly reading on with heart pounding
longing for connection and using words as a bartering
tool for love
A magnetized verbal emotional billboard cast wide to
see which listeners it will attract?

Just a means of expression in the claustrophobic
vacuum we struggle to break free of
At open poetry readings we use our words as life
savers, cast upon the waters looking for kindred
spirits to validate the ideas we hold sacred

Diamond in the Rough

You are a diamond in the rough
that was never nurtured and polished
you never made it out of the rough

Instead you carved out a small area around you
that let in an insufficient amount of sunlight
to reflect all you had to give
your imperfections were not addressed
and you were forced to accept a flawed view of
unperfected self

How sad, how very sad
you waited for the world
to be your savior
And you were already there
perfect as could be!

Subway Ride Going Home

Train going home
Stalled
Fat cop on the platform picking his teeth with a credit
card
Angry looking black woman
Seated middle aged man with swollen belly
looking eight months pregnant
moving
2nd Ave stop where I used to live 30 years ago
stalled
we wait we wait we wait
lock eyes with young woman in rust colored sweater
and scarf
she averts first, casts eyes downward
embarrassed
want to go home
we wait we wait we wait
finally
"Stand clear of the closing doors"

Mind Conversations

How much of our lives are governed by the internal
conversation?
Those imaginary talks we carry on with real others in
the world
We monkey chatter all the time to these friends,
family and strangers without uttering a single word
We are not crazy or deranged
and though these one way talks seem real enough,
occasionally we catch ourselves and realize, it's all in
our head

this rehearsal, this planning, this filler is not real at all
and yet we persist in this folly
whose motives are clearer if we step back a bit
But this further analysis is yet another level in the sub
basement of the here and now
A way of locking the latch to fresh air, light and true
consciousness
How to feel prepared or relaxed enough for what is
instead of fearing the misstep,
that we must talk this out while controlling both sides
of the conversation that rarely turns out to true
anyway!
So in reality, we are practicing for something that
most likely will not occur
Time and time again this falsehood is bore out and yet
we keep creating future scenes and unreal dialogue to
try and appease our lack of control
It is the stuff of dreams in our awake state,
no more real than a conversation with the dead
no more real than these writings,

just one person's internal thoughts without the benefit
of external feedback
not unlike this poem

Fuck You

Fuck you
Fuck you
It's my own fault
As I give you, I actually give you
the power of judging me

Who are you, that I care?
Am I so willing to trust your judgment over mine?
Is this just some cover, or reenactment of some
parental approval seeking?
Your nod, your love I think will give me worth
I'm more mature than that
Fuck you

America the Scam

The veneer of honesty
with the sordid underbelly
The repetitions of bait and switch played out over and
over
Dealt a losing hand so many times you accept this
only game in America
The fight and indignation pounded out of you
the rotten piece of pie we've come to not so secretly
believe is OK
Do unto others before they do unto you
The rules within the rules, the fine print, the
exception, the silent but
Just the way America does business
The straight face, the hoops, the jargon
all meant to cloud and distract you from what was
promised

The jaded shunted aside
to make more room for the uninitiated
two sets of books, two sets of rules

Yours free, America the scam

Marked down, once in a lifetime, going fast, money
back guarantee
America the scam
Buy now pay later, everyone's a winner, no one
turned away
America the scam
Am I telling you the truth or can I buy steal trick fool
or borrow your convictions

Hypocrite/Human

The less I know the more I'm sure what's right for
others
The more lost, confused, uncertain I am
the more apt I am to tell you exactly what to do
I can wantonly leer at the shapely behind of the young
woman fixing my morning coffee
and yet politely thank her with a genuine smile as she
hands me my change

I wade into the eddy of anxiety
unable to simply walk around it
while lacking the comprehension why others give in
to their vices
I blindly accept my narcissism, while detesting the
self centeredness of others

When my father lay dying I tried to bargain with God
Now if you ask me what I believe in,
I say softly, gravity alone

The ricocheting of beliefs and actions off one another
and ourselves is the sustaining life energy that
distracts and fascinates us
on this temporary merry go round of limited spins we
pretend not to count

Untitled

It's 6:35 a.m.
my wife is driving me to the bus
she drives slowly cautiously,
not yet in tune with the morn
the warmth from our bed quickly receding
in the unwarmed car
we made love silently in the middle of the night
words were not necessary than as now
as we try and put on a new day

Waiting

I am almost forty years older than you
how can I get you to see the prison walls of isolation
and unhappiness are built with your own hands?
I cannot lower the draw bridge to let you scamper
over the moat to Eden
You must through time, pain and measured efforts
struggle to find your own path
My explanations and examples annoy and embarrass
you to further despair
I hold up the mirror and you refuse to gaze at your
reflection, afraid of what you think you'll see
Your fear and shame masked in indifference and
apathy shackle your growing strength
Invisible hand cuffs of your own design restrict your
own participation in the pleasures to be had

I know my son for I once were you
And I wish to accelerate your sense of coming to
know yourself and the world better
But I can only wait, as I watch through the glass
unable to touch
as the see-saw of time uplifts you,
as I am lowered, closer to the ground
And I long for that sweet moment of equilibrium
when we will look each other in the eye
that day grows closer

September 2014 Cape May

Sitting at Sunset Beach Cape May, New jersey
Indian summer breezes mussing our hair
Fading summer sun, still warm enough to feel oh so
good
No children this trip
Victorian hotel stay, winery tour, boat ride, evening
theater, trivia night, seafood dining

Dwindling, dwindling summer
I wet my feet one last time in the choppy Atlantic
the sun is fading
we will leave soon
to face falling golden leaves and Autumn's chill

Mother at 86

If this poem were a picture, you would say it's to
large or the view to close
The details reveal too much, I chose a small area to
highlight that's out of context with the whole
But is that not the purpose of "art" to draw our
attention to the foreground and reveal what really is
there?

I hear the muted thump of a metal crutch,
the tip of which is covered to with rubber
It stabs the hardwood floor in my donated bedroom in
a measured sequence
The sound signifies my 86 year old mother is awake
How strange to now process this sound, replacing all
previous others to announce that my mother is up for
another day
She, who so many mornings ago used to rouse me, in
long forgotten manners
How this sound disturbs me, thump, thump, thump
It is the sound of longevity, infirmity, slowly feeling
our diminished way in the world
I admire her will and relative lack of complaint

She now laughs heartily at silly television shows
often repeating the punch line as she turns to me
hoping that I will laugh as deeply as she in a shared
moment
I do not remember this behavior in my younger
mother
Perhaps time, aging, simplifies things and previous
mysteries are distilled to fragile yet pure crystalline
truths?

I am not particularly close to my mother, guilt and
obligation long ago replaced my self righteous sense
of anger, hurt and longing
But these are not issues now, aging has changed the
terrain
A different set of dynamics is now in place
I do not laugh out loud with her at the funny lines
spoken on TV
And I am startled as she silently takes my hand in
hers, not sure what her gesture means
But sure that the deep under currents that run beneath
my consciousness are firmly embedded never to be
dislodged by time

Mother at 89

My 89 year old wheel chair bound mother resides in
an assisted living facility in West Orange, New Jersey
We try to visit once or twice a week for mutual
continuity
This past Saturday, a warm sunny early March day,
after a dreadful snowy cooped up in winter we took
her outside
To feel the comforting sun's rays teasingly promising
a new spring season to come

The piled snow receding like a glacier in glacial time
by the warming rays reveal a grass line like a show
girl tantalizingly lifting her hemline

We chat about the past week, the food, the lack of
privacy and the strange behavior of the, shall we say
aged clients, inmates, customers?
As we talk I notice the almost imperceptible drip,
drop by measured drop of the melting snow beside
my mother
The silent dripping like the ticking clock in a
Bergman film
The melting snow forms a hollowed out natural
bridge that will dissolve later when we are not there
I watch the melting snow, eye drop drips continually
programmed to drip, season by season, year by year,
life by life
And studying my mother's 89 year old face with her
swollen fingers and aged spotted hands
I do not forget the dripping ice is not measuring the
time for her alone

Brooklyn Revisited at 63

Visually skimming Brooklyn rooftops
on a now job related subway ride from Manhattan to a
Neptune Ave destination
via the NYC transit system
One sees, red brick schools, beige cinder block
buildings, eye level silver painted flat roofs
and Lego style apartment complexes framing Coney
Island the Cyclone ride in the distance

The majestic arching spanning silver grey Verrazano
not quite as spry as it was in 1964
opening up the wayward trek westward as Staten
Island residents are unable to hold back progress,
their once farmland and isolation overlaid with
asphalt and Brooklynites seeking better
One can only imagine Henry Hudson's thoughts
sailing into this once virgin territory
I think not he could foresee the potential harbor, the
ethnic migrations to follow, I think not,
auto body shops, pizza and bagel stores abounding in
this borough of churches
Contrasting architectural styles clash in the class
warfare struggle in confined close quarters

Russian, Chinese and other languages I can't
distinguish have transformed the former residents to
minority and aging resident status
I too am a tourist having left the nation's fourth
largest city for the so called Garden State, that was
supposed to be the natural progression of seeking
better

On this cool sunny breezy spring day, with the ocean
almost within sight, amorphous random thoughts of
childhood and youth are now analyzed with the
prospective lens of advanced middle age
Gone are the souls who formed my early
impressionable world's view, these ghosts only live
on in my buried synapses
the DNA doors to adult perception as solid as various
glimmering steel lines of track all converging at the
terminus

At the other end of Brooklyn a metamorphosis is
taking place
high priced towering condos and a resurgence of
youth and money invade, all seeking better
they transform once run down crime ridden areas of
long time neglect into something that is incongruent
to my long held comprehensions

I walk among these new, hip, changing
neighborhoods as feel as dazed as Henry Hudson
would, sailing his Half Moon ship up or down the
harbor for the first time

Chill in the Air

I tracked your ass as you minced across a cold
linoleum floor, one early October morning in 1975
It was in a tenement on the lower east side and the
landlord had yet to turn up the steam
Sweet guitar music of the time was the wall paper that
surrounded us
You wore a grey flannel night gown that clung to
your 20 something body in a way that wasn't fair, but
our hand held all the winning aces that day
We had little clue where we were going and were
happy in our insulated bubble of youthful desires
Our skin was thick to the world's erosion, pitfalls and
fears that were too slowly to blossom, that day they
were just seeds incubating below moist soil
Our vision was only up to our stunted horizon, not
realizing that decades later we would see well beyond
it, but never from the same room or together again
This is not a unique story,
and what made me recall this vision on a sunny
March day in 2012 while strolling down a crowded
Brooklyn Heights street was probably just, the chill in
the air

The Human Cry

In our forties we congratulated ourselves
on how good we looked and assumed it would
continue forever
In our sixties after menopause and graying and
thickening we knew the past was gone forever

Old enough to know right from wrong
which closed old familiar doors
and smart enough to avoid dangerous temptations that
will only momentary sate
We watch old age climbing over the picket fence
advancing towards us with nothing to do but stare it
in the eye and await the coming hand to hand grapple
that we will ultimately lose, like all those who have
gone before us

What have we learned that will help us now?
Awareness, acceptance, certainty?
We want more, the human cry

Untitled

You periodically draw forth and drink deeply from
your old reservoirs of pain and hurt for reasons
neither of us understand

What sends these emotions of hurt and anger hurling
into familiar orbits that seem to have a preordained
course to run?

Were they learned misinterpretations of a preverbal
child seeking order and logic in a chaotic maelstrom
of family dysfunction?

Are they hormonal tipping points that bay at the
moon, or needles that slip out of rational grooves due
to stress caused from life's protracted erosional
qualities?

Would understanding the cause prevent the wasted
energy and hurt that radiates out in a non productive
toxic haze of confusion that engulfs all within your
sphere?

This hollow paper tiger puffed up by innocuous
invented events spirals out of control to burn the
arsonist's hands as well

Tell me how to avoid/deflect these blows and
exaggerations that we both know are insincere and
temporary, yet leave emotional marks and bruises?

How best to quickly return to the road of equilibrium?
We need a map that can be trusted, not one that goes
in circles and needlessly injures the explorers

Waiting

My wife's demeanor is quiet and withdrawn
She doesn't start the same petty arguments, or smile
as easily
Her inner focus has shifted, I am no longer on the
radar screen
A vacant blip, blip, blip fails to register the inner
turmoil
She goes about her activities with a cool sure
efficiency masking the massing anxiety of the ever
approaching abyss
Her mother of 86 has been diagnosed with colon
cancer
We await the doctor's decision as to when to operate
The Brooklyn hospital struggles with the balancing
act of economics verses patient care and seems to lose
its footing without evening blushing
My wife's siblings and relatives are drawn into the
vortex of confronting mortality and assume their
proper roles of responsibility
Their axes have been tilted off kilter in a suspended
moment of time that has lasted ten days
A large collected inhale is waiting to be exhaled in
relief or dread
As age, illness and modern medicine collide in the
fate of a mother who's 86 years of life's ripples, touch
many distant shores
and now balances in the ether between here and there

I Spoke to God Last Night

I spoke to God last night
It was only in a dream
I awoke suddenly and could only recall a few details
A woman was in great pain and God was responsible
Don't ask me how I knew this, this was my dream
I said to God "You better stop now or you won't look
so good in your own eyes"
The gravity of my reproach shocked me to
consciousness in the darkness
Do those that believe in God believe in peer review?
Does God ask, "How am I doing?"
How many stars does he get, can we trade him/her for
another/
"You better stop now or you won't look so good in
your own eyes" How's that for a UN slogan, how's
that for a moral code?
A pause to reflect
"You better stop now or you won't look so good in
your own eyes"
If only uttered over history, to shame the shameful
into higher moral action
To pause the powerful to reassess, to pause the
powerful to reassess, to pause the powerful to
reassess

From Here to There

Where to go from here?
The old and familiar are worn and faded, lacking in
current and currency
The new is unborn, out of reach just a hungry concept
How to invent new future without a map, with age
and depression exerting drag upon the wheels of
change?
I look for familiar faces among the crowd of strangers
whose passions now confuse me
tick tock, tick tock, unsavory inertia shackles the soul
in the fog before me
Hoping, knowing, the sunshine behind this mist is as
real as the current quagmire
I blame no one, as I search the shed for tools to slip
from here to there

Who Was That Pretty Girl...?

Who was that pretty girl watching television with our
son in the basement?

Yesterday my wife and I met our 20 year old son's
first serious girlfriend
We had heard snippets of information about her in the
last several weeks
as he disappeared for days on end with comments
like, I'm staying at school or dorm or with friends, or
at M's house

Our son previously declining my wife's request to
invite her over
Why this Sunday does she appear, we do not know
Some minimal, muted announcement of M's stopping
by before returning to her dorm
Could it be **her curiosity to meet us,** to
learn more about the boy she's "seeing"?
Could it be some non verbal evidence of our son's
maturing process,
his seeking our approval, testing our reaction,
metaphorically showing us that they seesaw is now
almost level?

Who was that pretty girl eating dinner with us at our
table?
Who is this attractive stranger with the bright eyes
and expressive personality?
Should we offer her wine or beer, pleasantly relieved
at her reply "that soda is fine"

Slightly awkward banter about our son's proclivities
and gentle family traits are revealed as we seek some
common ground of satisfying curiosity
My wife and I are silently impressed by her grounded
pragmatic sense and easy laugh
We also clearly witness a side of our son previously
hidden from view
Later, I call "good night" down the stairs as my wife
and I prepare for bed.
and traveling back up the stairs (of passing time) is an
unfamiliar pretty feminine voice saying "good night,
it was a pleasure meeting you"

House of Cards?

A man and a woman meet
and go on a date

Over time the relationship is cobbled together with
brick and lust
Over time he reveals his business plan
Over time she signs the papers
The deal is sealed
The marriage begins with clear unspoken agreements
Acquiescence to let the man lead
Acquiescence to let the man call the shots
Acquiescence to follow

Over time the woman grows resentful
Over time she wants to modify the plan
Over time she doesn't want what she once wanted

The man is confused
He has gotten his way for so long
He does not sense the gathering wind
The gale that scatters the straw,
that once was brick and lust
all over their now harvested field

Between

My 18 year old son lives at home
It is the summer between high school ending and
college beginning
He is between boy and man
Still tethered to us his parents, all knowing,
experienced and sure
Yet eager to break away and follow his own instincts
The frustration overflows in surly volcanic eruptions
of rudeness and outright anger
How do you hold on and let go at the same time?
A reoccurring theme in life, difficult to master
Yet played out time and time again

We his parents and boy man or man boy were at the
beach
A place he is still, strangely comfortable being seen
with us
At the water's edge, I ask him-
"What do you do when you want to do something and
no one else does?"
He tentatively replies "You do it by yourself?"
That question mark at the end of his reply reveals late
adolescence uncertainty

He then asked me if I was going into the surf?
A bit too cold for this 56 year old I replied
After a bit of reluctance he waded in and dove under
an incoming wave

Small parental pleasures are deeply acknowledged by
such simple acts

Best Seller?

I'm reading your novel
You know the one that won all those awards
It's 500 pages and covers just four days
Am I supposed to like the protagonist?
Am I supposed to identify with him,
find him, cerebral, funny, humane, everyman?

I don't

You skill which is vast,
is like a two inch wide vein of golden ore
snaking around the innards of a 500 ton mountain
I see the wealth but it's not worth the mining
Good luck
I'm off to the seaside

Coffee Cup of Time

I decided to hand wash out a coffee cup and dispense
with the dishwasher
I rinsed the cup and turned it upside down at eye level
over the sink to let the excess water drain off
And like life, the runoff, liquidation of time and
energy slowed, ebbed from splash, to trickle to rapid
drops to slower drops

Each drop forming by the pull of gravity, sliding to
the exact same departure point and slowly free falling
into the sink below

Each drop collecting markedly slower than the one
before

One silently wonders, just how many drops are left,
because logic dictates there must be a finite amount

And yet we are amazed by how wrong we are, as the
drops keep forming slower and slower and slower
misguidedly tricking us into thinking the drops are
endless

My patience wanes and I place the still wet cup in the
draining board
and utilize my ever diminishing time with hardly a
conscious thought

Who's Winning, Who's Counting

My wife wants me to cut the universe some slack
Why hold a grudge when you can't change things?
Things will break, people will be stupid and violent
We will suffer pain, humiliation and boredom
Prices will go up, quality may not
We will always ask why?
We might try pushing that rock up the hill in futility
We push, we grunt, we curse but we keep on pushing
for us
The universe is not keeping score
The scoreboard is only in our mind

Toast

I am a slice of bread from the loaf of baby boomers
I was born in the 1950's and attended PS so and so in
Brooklyn or the Bronx or where ever
Some seminal cultural touch points are, Catcher in the
Rye, West Side Story, Death of a Salesman, On The
Waterfront, Mighty Mouse, Bob Dylan, The Beatles,
the Kennedy assassination, Watergate
Need I go on? You get the point
We are locked in a generation of shared cultural and
historical events that separate us from our parents and
our children
Is it comforting or lonely to have our special
memories?
We are moving to the back of the record bin (as if
there is a current record bin) with deceased or aging
parents, slipping down that slippery slope as we
watch, first hand up close, unable to halt that trip to
oblivion

I said good bye to my 80 something mother the other
day after a visit to help her fill out some simple forms
that vexed her
When leaving, she stood at the door with unspoken
worry, fear and death in her eyes
With the same innocent world vulnerability of the
young girl she once was when protected by the
illusion of strong loving parents
Now the circle closes, as we are told it should
The bread grows staler as the loaf diminishes before
being toasted
Dust to breadcrumbs, breadcrumbs to dust
We return to whence we came, who remembers us?

Allegiance

Is my allegiance, to my wife, my son, my brother, my
country, my ego, my gender, my age, my race, my id,
to truth, that snake like line that slithers to and fro

Is this allegiance like a new set of clothes, changed on
a daily basis and appropriately washed and ironed
depending on the occasion it is to be presented?

How conveniently without apparent contradiction do
we shift the tumblers, reset the allegiance, to assuage
our place in the world?

When inspected too closely we risk paralysis and
when challenged by others we shift so smoothly to
the safe harbor of rationalization

The auto pilot of pride masks turbulent injustices we
do not seek to acknowledge, least it reveal the flawed
individuals that shame us, should the mirror be held
up

We are skilled at distorting the image revealed,
denying the vision as misplaced atoms

This vain sense of self too fragile and nervous to sit at
the table with our other poker playing players, all
trying to game the system of life

The Painted Gate

It's time to repaint the old gate as the elements have taken their toll. Cracked and chipped paint is in need of repair to prevent further rotting and decay. After carefully prepping and sanding it's time to apply a "new coat" of white paint. I am always eager to begin the first brush stroke. I broadly apply the paint with a two inch wide brush repainting the same surface that some anonymous, person to me painted some years ago. I retrace his hand with fresh paint, hoping to recreate the same fresh new look that he had accomplished. What thoughts went through his mind as he spread the paint evenly over the grain? Will the next painter notice how carefully and precisely I painted the tiny areas by the hinges Will they care? Will they think my work substandard? We, painters of gates notice the nuances that the common observer overlooks. Decisions of detail are made on an individual basis. Do I paint the underside? Do I take the time to use a thinner brush to get into those tight spaces? We, painters of gates, unconsciously share a conversation without words that span the years. What is communicated by that old paint spot on the ground? Do I wash away all my mistakes? And when the paint job is finished, if done properly, no one will really notice as it will blend into the context as it should. No one will really notice, except the next painter (as we silently nod to each other through the gate). And he will have the last word.

One Day You Wake Up and You're 62

One Day You Wake Up and You're 62
And though you knew it was coming, the arrival
catches you off guard, like an unexpected emotional
inhale
An idle bobbing of a self imposed buoy on the ocean
voyage meant to designate direction

Last night I dreamt I was practicing for an upcoming
baseball season,
while lounging in uniform, on shaded park benches, I
told my fellow players I wanted to lose five pounds
and to my chagrin they said they wanted to end
practice early to avoid injuries
Even my unconscious is wrestling with desire and
moderation
Another season, always hoping for another season
To peak ahead and learn what will transpire while
suspending our youth in glorious limbo

By 62 you've been around the block, a Magellan of
navigating relationships, marriage, desire and loss
You've probably tasted some very good wine, made
some money lost some money, not to mention, broken
bones, kidney stones, hemorrhoids a little osteo and
hopefully not too much more than a scare or two
You might have lost a parent or two, and known a
few cancer victims and survivors
The ever hardening plaster of personality, that is so
much more difficult to flex
The ever greater acceptance/nonacceptance of others
The inner voice acknowledging that, "what we want,
we want" is slipping beyond our grasp

72 seems a lot closer than 52
82 is within the realm of possibility
We are ignorant of how this all came to pass, the
mind excited, confused and perhaps a little wary of
what portends
With the added wisdom comes the knowledge of the
closing doors and the nearer horizon
Regrets abound, unfulfilled potential, wasted time,
and hypothetical do over's
if you dwell too long in the land of "what ifs"

The pleasures seem sweeter and the savoring is
enhanced by the awareness of alternatives and the
dwindling time
The frustrations of the world dilemma are too vast to
comprehend and hopefully offset by the awareness of
goodness in others,
and boundless curiosity propels us forward for as far
as the life force can propel us

Celebrate, celebrate for isn't that what we're here for!

Twilight Worries Between Sleep & Wakefulness

And now I'm left to argue with dust
if I care to
The damage done
Chicken or egg, genetic, organic or learned?
Mother, when I was young, you held my forehead
when I vomited
that is not love enough
Father where were you, out chasing your narcissistic
appetites?
We played out our failing roles
The emotional scaffold you provided was too weak to
support me
How could your child be so unworthy?
Was I not worth the effort?
Why couldn't you reach me, how hard did you try?
Who were the parents and who was the child?
Were you tortured souls doing the best you could?
I limp on attempting to sidestep invisible potholes
that swallow me up as the road narrows
Who can help me now, when I can't help myself?
What good to argue with dust?
What direction to turn to now, the compass broken

Came to an Age

Came to an age when I prefer to sit in the shade rather
than the hot summer sun
Became the family patriarch not by attaining wisdom
or skill but by merely surviving
When you wear the clothes long enough they begin to
fit and feel comfortable
You might delude yourself into thinking the crown
fits, unlike my younger days filled with timidity,
when I thought the world was my judge and I plead
guilty to every imagined offense
One learns to take the long view and to look to the
horizon rather than the emotional foreground
Forgive my reflectiveness for
my mother died last week

Life?

Oh I get the big picture, birth, growing up, maturity, adulthood, work, maybe marriage children, celebrations, milestones, slow decline maybe disease and finally death. I just don't get the nuances in between, or maybe I get the nuances but not the big picture.

Life is a constant adjustment to figuring it all out as the plates you stand on continue to spin at various speeds on different planes. Maybe best not to think too much or one can become quite disoriented, what to keep foreground and what to keep background. It's impossible to keep it ALL in focus at one time, the lens isn't wide enough. The internal syllabus somehow keeps the plant secured to the stake to collect the most sun and prevent the vine from wandering to places that are dark and dank. Sometimes the blueprints get a little smudged and strange irregularities pop up.
On the bright side we call it artistic expression or novel creativity of the soul. On the dark side, a loose rope railing we struggle to grasp as we try and not fall into the abyss.

It's all quite encompassing and always fascinating whether going up or down the mountain

Five Words to Sum up Life

Have I got your attention?
Have I peaked your curiosity?
And the answer is- "Life is what it is"
Because of a crack in my emotional foundation or an
over active amygdala or a curious mind
I search for a unified theory of why?

Whether you smile or cry, life is what it is
You can, not go gently into that good night with
Dylan Thomas or quote Kurt Vonnegut's "So it goes"
You can wail or flail, or moan and groan with Doctor
Seuss
You can stand up and shout, or lay down and die
It all means everything or it all means nothing
Expand the ego to the size of the universe or shrink it
to the pre big bang atom
Experience it to the max or shrivel up into a catatonic
ball
Yet, life is what it is
Five words to sum up existence
Some will find solace with this
and some won't But life is what it is
Spend your time thinking and analyzing this or spend
your life doing or not doing
life is what it is
A simple concept you say, a cliché, a cop out
Try living it, without judgment, approval or
disapproval, it doesn't care
Life is what it is
Acceptance of reality, far beyond the self, neither
good nor bad, so hard to accept, life is what it is

I posit this not out a sense of surrender or futility or
rationalization or resignation, but of acceptance
Life is what it is
Some may find this deep as an ocean or shallow as a
puddle but life is, what it is

Upon some reflection I realize I could have titled this
poem,
Death of a friend

Another Retirement Party

The conveyer belt of time transports my generation to
the next station of life,
descending or ascending depending upon
your persuasion
More than a quarter century of a man's life being put
aside,
voluntarily severing the roots of everyday
acquaintances and acquired routines for vast stretches
of unmoored time,
with the freedom to lose one's wristwatch without
accountability
To reenter the endless summer of childhood before
institutions and bureaucracies beckoned
To frolic and play with the wisdom of all your
worldly experiences firmly in place and your front
door wide open
This is the payoff, to eagerly embrace a new path
provisioned with a small knap sack of acquired
experience that is worth far more than gold
You hold the compass in your hand
and step forward to see what will happen

Fish Have No Hands

Now you have read my poems
You know me; I have revealed myself to you
the reader, the voyeur

Who is better for it?

You the reader, who has come to know a stranger, up
close and personal without leaving your easy chair or
perhaps your bed
Have you been pleased?
Was the time well spent?
Were you bored, put off, could not relate?
You have formed your opinions that I'll never know
But that's not really important

I the naked fisherman have thrown the net of myself
upon the sea
I slowly retrieve the net with salt water gushing
through the open box like twine
capturing the briny experience that is, the seaweed,
the flapping fish with receding life, the multi colored
shells, the garbage
We are all fisherman tending our seas as best we can,
like fish with no hands
Trying to master our environment with inadequate
means
Struggling for purpose and settling for emotional
connection to guide us through our brief time upon
the water
So reader, thank you, for you have served me well, in
my need of an audience, whether real or imagined

Take some comfort that by reading this you know we
are compatriots
like silent voices in the wind all flowing in the same
direction

Stories

Rejected by *The New Yorker*

It was time to submit a story to *The New Yorker* magazine. Why the hell not? He was 63 years old and had never published a single story or poem in over 40 years of scribbling down his inner most thoughts. He had not attended the acclaimed Iowa program of writing, was not an English literature major in college, nor did he aspire to any master's writing program in some city or state university. Being self taught and a reflective person who had consumed a lifetime of serious literature as well as more than his share of pop, pulp printed material he felt there must be a modest place in this world for his printed life perceptions and interpretations via poem or story. He knew the work, pain and joy of translating an idea or thought from mind to the harsh light of paper, to see if it didn't transform to mush and pablum. So he decided to present his best story to the prestigious *New Yorker* magazine despite his last name not being Beattie or Updike, and let the chips fall where they may.

Always attentive to listening to authors serious reflections on their craft whether on Charlie Rose, NRP radio or some other media outlet, he hoped to glean some practical or mystical secret that would be the alchemy to turn his musings into gold. He was always left with the plain realization that writers must "just write". Water seeks its own level as they say. But do writers find their readers in some equivalent fashion? How many new books constantly populate the literary landscape, whether on Amazon, eBooks or that ever -scacer brick and mortar store? New books with their latest graphically designed covers seemed to flourish with the frequency of never ending new wine labels constantly multiplying on the shelves of liquor stores. Like mushrooms sprouting after a summer rain, weeds in a garden, it was impossible not to be bombarded by new literature. It couldn't all be good for every reader. But is there not a lid for every jar?

He knew he could spin a phrase, rearrange words or concepts in an interesting or thought provoking manner. Are not the reflections of a serious 63 year old worth something to some segment of the reading world? How not to collect some interesting observations that must be of some value to some readers after having been around the block a time or 10,000?

How about the lines-
"When my father lay dying I believed in bargaining with God. Now if you ask me what I believe in, I say softly, only gravity." Or perhaps "This ricocheting of beliefs and actions off one another and ourselves is the sustaining life energy that distracts and fascinates us on this temporary merry go round of limited spins we pretend not to count." Or on the whimsical side, "It was a dark and stormy night in hipster Williamsburg Brooklyn."
Does this not cause a contemplative inquisitive reader to ask for more, to raise an eyebrow and provoke an "um I'm hungry?"

Not having an agent, he unsuccessfully submitted numerous literary pieces to various outlets, many free some paid, all seductively seeking unpublished authors to apply. Hence after unsuccessfully feeding this nebulous invisible world of writer's heaven with his best material, he was left with that isolated feeling that he alone was not told the password that would grant access to that secret world of the gloriously published.

So a writer writes and like the myth of Sisyphus he continues to submit his labor of love to those who seem to have, turned away faces and ears covered with mittened hands. So he slaved away on his very best short story, editing and rewriting drafts over and over. He polished and buffed each individual word until he saw his own reflection smiling back at him. He insightfully depicted several universal themes in new and clever post-Freudian analytical terms.

For example, the sumo wrestling match between love and lust with his main character fighting with a meta-physical hand tied behind his back (and his thong slipping). Or the universal theme defended, whereby children believe their parents are aged dolts and resist drinking or even sipping from the fountain of knowledge unconditionally offered up for fee.

And who has mastered, the old age of youth or as we like to call it, the new 65? All this and more in the post hipster period of Brooklyn in the 2020's offered up freely to the editors of *The New Yorker* just for the taking.

He caressed, bathed and powdered the wonderful little

offspring of his intellect. He wrapped it in pretty paper, tied with a bow, clearly destined in his mind to smash open the door to the world of published by its sheer weight of talent, thereby bypassing the need of the afore mentioned password, used only by the connected. Charlie Rose would interview him in prime time as well as Bill Moyers. Asking how could America have overlooked such a natural talent for so so long? Ann Pachett would call seeking tips on writing and finally he would preemptively receive next year's National Book Award because it was clear no literary light on the horizon shone brighter.

But alas no, his story was rejected by *The New Yorker*, like thousands before and thousands to come by other unknown authors. Was he dejected? Did he harbor feelings of anger, rage and slight? No. But what is a writer to do, but write for that's what we are, writers in search of an audience of more than one. We wish to vindicate our voice in the wind, whether we learn the password or not.

He took out a clean white page to begin again.

The End
(or just the beginning)

The Sand Box

This is not an unusual story. It's about four adults,
two suburban families, one infidelity and the mind set
of an aggrieved husband. Tom and Mary Calducci
and their 15 year old son, Matt, lived next door to
Andy and Joan Burton with their two children, 14
year old Andy Jr., and the pleasant surprise /mistake,
or should I say, the unplanned now 3 year old Annie.
Andy had built for Annie a sandbox to play in when
she was 2. It took several trips to Home Depot and
several long hours under a hot July sun to construct
sand and stain the rectangular play area. The sandbox
was four feet by six feet, about the size of a large
mattress or a cemetery plot. On the surface, one might
say, there flourished a solid friendship of
superficiality between the two families. The
Calducci's and the Burton's would entertain each
other with backyard barbecues. The men would drink
pale ales while the women favored white wine. Tom
and Andy would take the boys to baseball games in
the summer and hockey games in the winter. Mary
and Joan would go shopping at the mall or take little
Annie to the movies or the town frozen yogurt store
where you selected your own toppings. Once, the two
families rented a house for a week "down the Jersey
shore", as they say. Nothing is remarkable about any
of the central characters, as normal as normal is.

One might say they never broke through to the inner
circle of confidences, except for Andy and Mary.
Their affair was the usual kind, tinged with betrayal,
excitement, sexual and otherwise, tension, guilt and

longing. It began about a year ago. Mary, bored and feeling unappreciated, felt Andy Burton's gentle sensitive footprint on the earth perfectly overlapped hers and provided a snug comfortable fit, very compatible to her true nature. To complete the metaphor, Mary felt her husband Tom wore cleats on golf shoes that tore at the earth and left divots that he never replaced. In her mind he lacked a certain sensitivity and when they first dated she accepted this as maleness and self confidence. Let other people replace the divots, never the mess they left behind. As the years gathered momentum, she now saw his actions as insensitive, reckless and self-centered. At first Tom suspected the infidelity. He caught their glances that lasted a tad too long. He saw fleeting touches that triggered long ago memories when, while dating Mary, they had visited her parents in the mountains for a weekend stay. He tried to hide his overt longings from his bride -to- be, from her parents. Over time he knew his suspicions to be valid, no catching them in the act was necessary. He let the charade proceed for a while. He quietly and stoically suffered the pain and hurt as he tried to understand the situation. Was it some failing on his part? Was it random circumstances of flawed people in close proximity to each other? Was it the human condition of imperfect genes, institutions of moral learning, schools, families, religious groups that failed to provide the moral fiber that keeps society together? Did it matter? A confidence, security, trusts had been ripped from him. Tom Calducci wanted to feel whole again. Revenge, as old as the bible, would feel justified and provided a bromide for a wounded, now tortured, soul. I could pad this story with superfluous details of what the characters looked like or what they did, or even how Mary and Andy were almost caught one late night at the beach. Would that draw you the reader closer to liking or despising the central characters of this story? Would these details touch your life in some way, to rationalize the characters' behavior in your mind? Well never mind, this is Tom's story.

Tom being a somewhat educated, tortured man with tunnel vision, designed a plan. Of course, he could have confronted his wife and duplicitous friend Andy. But that was not what he wanted.

He did not want to feel superior. He could not undo the doable. There is no reset. There is no unmemorying. He wanted revenge. He did not care what happened to him, or his son or Joan or Andy Jr. or little Annie. It was a very simple uncomplicated plan. At some point he would drug his wife and Andy. Once they were unconscious, he would drag their comatose bodies to the sand box near the shed and remove the sand by shovel. He would place their bodies side by side in the 4 x 6 foot previously described mattress/cemetery plot and add the appropriate amount of quick drying cement, using the backyard garden hose to attain the proper consistency. From the basement he would get the trowel and smoothly spread the quick drying cement as if icing on a cake. The former sand box, now a cement mattress or coffin, encasing an adulterous couple, would become a tomb forever invisible to the world.

Well that was Tom's plan. It helped ease him back to sleep when he awoke at three a.m. with feelings of rage as Mary slept peacefully beside him. Tom went so far as to calculate just how much quick drying cement he would need. He checked the Internet for available powerful "date rape" drugs that would do the trick.

As you may recall, I began this story by saying it was not an unusual one and I am a man of my word. Tom Calducci did not murder his wife or his neighbor Andy Burton. In fact, Tom did not even divorce Mary. There were in fact many tears shed, much screaming and yelling, counseling sessions both individual and as a couple. There was also a trial separation that failed. But, in the end, Tom and Mary sold their house and moved to Florida. Mary and Andy never spoke to each other again. Joan and Andy did, in fact, get divorced. Who knows what tips the scales enough in favor or not, in terms of staying together? There is just no predicting. Annie outgrew her sand box and all the children grew up reasonably well. Tom and Mary soldiered on with an indiscretion that could be tolerated, but not wholly overcome. That was their choice. As I said in the beginning, this was not an unusual story.

The End

Letters

Earlier that day Jack had happened upon some old
letters from Pam and Barbara. He reread them slowly
and old memories were recalled with energy and life.
How two women who had never met, who had
nothing in common except landing on the "same
square" at different points in time had arrived at the
same conclusion. From different views they saw or
felt the incompleteness, the longing for what was
unattainable. It took them different lengths of time to
acquire such disappointing wisdom. And though
Barbara severed the rope faster and recovered
quicker, who's to say the damage wasn't as costly to
Pam who transversed a greater emotional distance?
The letters were of four and five years ago. Some
spoke of joy, sharing and anticipation. They recalled
going to Washington DC to see a Renoir exhibit, to
Montreal for a long weekend. Some of the yellowing
letters expressed the happiness and satisfaction of
spending an afternoon in bed together, sedate with
sexual bliss, as the cooing of pigeons on the fire
escape filtered out the city traffic below. The tone of
the letters changed gradually as if running some
predetermined course. So that by the end, the letters
attacked the mind's senses as if emerging from a cool
dark movie theater onto a bright traffic congested
avenue on a humid August afternoon. One was jarred
to face a new reality. The letters spoke of accusations,
betrayals, pleadings and finally bitterness and
goodbyes. The letters had been kept all these years.
Why, proof, proof that women had cared, a tally of
broken hearts? Jack put a rubber band back around
the stack of letters and returned them to the back of

the bottom draw of a cluttered desk in the spare bedroom. As if this remoteness would protect him from his past actions.

Jack spent the afternoon listlessly meandering from room to room waiting for Diane to call. They hadn't spoken in three days. At 4 p.m. he decided to call her. The ring sounded distant, and after six rings when he knew she was not answering he let it ring on and on. Finally Jack hung up, combed his hair, grabbed his keys from the kitchen counter and headed for the door. In the lobby he checked his mailbox and found a solitary letter waiting for him. It was addressed to his Christen name in Diane's handwriting. Diane had always used his nickname after their first date. Jack stood motionless for a long moment. Then as if in slow motion he removed a book of matches from his breast pocket and lit the lower right corner of the envelope.

It burned quickly as he dropped it in the sand of the half used ash tray by the elevator. Jack was disoriented as he walked out onto the hot humid bright city street.

The End

Arc of a Memory

Awakened at 3 a.m. by bolt- like anxiety that erupts
from the teeming unconscious of decades of stored
memories and experiences. It now manifests itself in
undefined ill at ease, with no clear handle but
symptoms never the less.

In the dark predawn hours, my mind searched for a
distraction to tamp down the nausea and panic of
unresolved whatever. Seeking to find solace I recalled
a long ago memory rekindled by a chance encounter
the day before, of woman from my past.

Almost thirty years ago when I was 30 I met a foreign
born mother 27 of immense beauty who had been cast
adrift by divorce. Once on 34th street she asked me
what size breasts I'd preferred. Once riding the
subway with her I was almost unable to contain
myself, the urge so strong to explode polite
conversation with a lunging, lust driven passionate
kiss. So powerful was her pull to silence my words
and hijack my senses. This effect was not lost on me
alone, as all men were drawn into the gravitational
pull of her allure. And this "advantage" she used to
her maximum, not in a cruel fashion but more like an
attention addiction, constantly needing male attention
to confirm her desirability. The revelation of defects
and insecurities she hid shallowly beneath her surface
were more than I wished or hoped to take on. I not
wanting or worthy of the glare, preferring the
shadows, but it was impossible not to be awed by the
starburst that illuminated all males before her. Her

friendliness was a deal. It gave all men hope of attaining her and buffeted her sense of worth. I thought. I've watched from a distance the arc of her life, professional success, and long loyal female friendships. Her male relationships drifted and evolved from unstable to volatile to finally a stable quieter long standing marriage.

As I said earlier I randomly encountered her on the street yesterday. She had grown somewhat matronly with expanding crow's feet about the eyes. She seemed more relaxed, perhaps weary of the games and rules we self impose upon ourselves. In fact she seemed slightly annoyed by the attention of a casual male acquaintance that happened to be with her and interrupted our conversation several times. But she was never rude and indulged him to a small extent.

It is said that as we age our traits become amplified, but some are also diminished and refined. Perhaps I've misread the circumstances and my own defects and insecurities have colored my perceptions. Yet recalling these distant details had quelled my anxieties and relaxed my psyche. I was able to return to sleep with no regrets.

The End

Shoveling (Blizzard of Sunday Dec. 26, 2010)

In the aftermath, on Monday morning, 24 inches of
drifting snow blankets and clogs the streets and
byways of northern New Jersey. I venture out through
our garage, wearing ski pants, hat, scarf, sweatshirt,
overcoat and gloves. As gale force wind affirms the
adage, "you don't spit into the wind". I'm pelted in the
face with fine powered snow. At first glance, viewing
the drifts, rising as high as the car's windows and the
densely packed plowed in the end of the driveway,
my initiative sinks and thoughts of retreat abound in
this almost 60 year old well- layered ex athlete. Then
the sight and sounds of neighbors, mostly male,
shoveling and snow blowing their way to freedom
(clearing the path for their SUV's to hit the road)
makes me take up my shovel and join the male
mission of rejecting cabin fever and regaining access
to the greater world beyond. I begin shoveling and
unlike previous years I must pause more frequently
than ever to catch my breath. I frequently remove my
gloves to flex frozen fingers back to life. My running
nose leaves a damp handkerchief in my pocket as
well as drizzling the surrounding snow in my
immediate circumference. After a few minutes I
question why my son is still sleeping and why my
neighbors with their noisy snow blowers don't come
to their older beleaguered over whelmed neighbor's
aid? Did I offend then in some way? I will not whine.
I will not complain. I decide to resent them all and
use my anger to press on. Slowly and incrementally I
make progress, having to work the same area two or
three times as the snow is that deep.

You need to lop off the upper section first, then go back for the lower half. I get into the job, gaining a strength, rhythm and pace- me against the elements. I look up and admire the bright blue sky and it's quickly "whited out" by another mighty gust that seems to recreate the original blizzard. I turn my body sideways and look downward until the gale subsides and the stinging white powder stops hitting my face. It feels good and purposeful to work so hard (but so much more to go). Suddenly my next door neighbor appears, snow blower in tow. He tells me that he and another neighbor were clearing the path and driveway of yet another neighbor who was away on vacation. He quickly steps in with his snow eating monster and devours the remaining thick snow wall that had sealed the end of our driveway, previously plowed in by the town. The smell of gasoline hangs in the air as the snow is shot high in the sky, the fine particles caught in the wind drifting towards the next far off driveway. How could I ever doubt the essential goodness on my neighbors, I guiltily ask myself? When the end of the driveway is cleared I thank my neighbor after discussing snow blower prices (mentally noting it's time for such a purchase) and we each resume our tasks. I am encouraged and renewed as I work on clearing the drifts around and between our three cars. Where once the job seemed endlessly hopeless, I now see that I can finish the job myself. This a pattern played out time and again in my life. A little self constructed game where I trick myself into a feeling of accomplishment and pride by overcoming a "great obstacle" that was self erected or over estimated at first. A little more shoveling and the driveway is just about done. I'm feeling good now, warm proud and enjoying the day. I could stop now, no one would say I should do more. I've made my mark apparent for all to see. Instead of going in, I want more. Mother Nature called me out and here I am! I decide to take on the task of clearing the walkway from the front door to the driveway. I start with clearing the steps and begin creating a trench or erecting snow walls on either side of me about four feet apart. The wind is muffled by my hood, my hands and fingers are comfortable and warm, perspiration keeps my trunk loose and limber. Slowly I proceed trying to find the pavers under the thick blanket of snow as my guide. I frequently wander off course clearing parts of the lawn by accident. I pause and look around. It's mid afternoon. The neighbors are done and have gone inside, not a sole to be seen. I feel alone in the elements.

What if I had a heart attack, who would know, who would find me and when? If I collapsed and slowly went to sleep between these pristine white snow walls, this tunnel without a roof, with the wind howling around me and the bright blue sky above (and the path almost finished), what then? Would that be a bad death? I cut short the thought and resume shoveling. My wife comes out and asks "how much longer?" "Don't be a martyr come in." I reply "a little more I want to finish." Later I will come in, wordlessly pass my son (with his head cold) napping on the couch with his girlfriend. I will take two aspirin and wearily sit down next to wife, sipping a can of coke with a far away distant look in my eyes. She will ask what time I want dinner, but I will be thinking, I'm spent, and I left too much of myself outside today. But I cleared another walkway, beat another storm and enjoyed almost every minute of it immensely.

The End

Haiku's

Depression is the
indent of your sad spirit
you accept as real

Love can rebound if
there's a hard wall to echo
desire within

The past is long gone
the present is all we have
dwell not far ahead

God's presence is in
the breath within the breath or
so we like to think

Later for you man
the A train silently calls
my joyful trek home

Love is in the wind
a stillness may turn to gale
must we wait the change

It is your sweet sigh
that is all I have to hear
to celebrate life

The phone does not ring
the silence is not welcome
where is my lover

Blood trickles slowly
from the wounded players cut
how real this moment

The ball rose skyward
as the crowd inhaled as one
time is suspended

How do we awake
from the self inflicted sleep
of our selfish life

How do we awake
from the perceived sleepy haze
of distorted lies

How do we shed the
misery of the black box
we chose to live in

We struggle to free
the colorful butterfly
we have just netted

Life continues on
we seek dissonance of both
old and new to meld

We walk in circles
thinking we are moving on
is this not the truth

Brooklyn could be the
center of the universe
for those in the know

Haiku for you Fran
to brighten your day with words
until flesh be kissed

Words are limited
to express what I feel in
seeing your sweet smile

Here I sit and wait
bidding my time in service
I must so endure

When my sentence ends
then I am free to seek a
brand new prison cell

Forgive my writing
and spelling and my grammar
father taught English

Unable to see
beyond my experience
I must trust others

The cosmic truths lie
beyond the outer reach of
none who will question

Focus on the breath
all else will dissolve away
leaving only now

The hunger in me
lasts a life time to be sure
will you dine with me

My glasses distort
light rays entering my brain
so that I can see

Squeeze out a haiku
like Crest toothpaste from a tube
neither can go back

Actor with a dry
sense of humor could perhaps
be a ham on wry

Round and round we go
rarely breaking the circle
that we so despise

Round and round we go
loving perfect symmetry
we love the worn path

The pebble in the
shoe that is so annoying
brings us great pleasure

It never pauses
the eternal clock of life
fear not the alarm

Awake from a dream
to realize it is a dream
we are living in

The opiate sleep
so powerful in its tug
like the ocean tide

Life's conversation
goes beyond mere words being
the wind of time

Running like the wind
fast as you can, your youth is
running right beside

Anti-depressants
to keep perspiration off
the so worried brow

Thank goodness moods change
that is the hope of the sad
if remembered

As one gets older
it's so easy to find fault
with what we hold dear

To replace the no
with positive yeses is
our endless goal

You have to laugh at
the joy we rob ourselves of
in the guise of truth

Create formula
not yet discerned, could make
you a wealthy man

Who will stand up for
principle over money
only a saint or a fool

To speak so fast and
surf the mind so swiftly is
a ride of pleasure

Think of yourself as
a huge mountain sitting as
still as an idea

As one grows older
death's shore is growing closer
don't avert the eyes

Being a parent
you join a club that opens
the heart to so much

Being a parent
you join a club that opens
the circle again

Being a parent
you join a club that allows
resting of the self

The track of friendship
roller coasters through decades
careening along

Pre dawn thoughts and dreams
vanish like a water mirage
in the morning light

What is consciousness?
but a tape that plays forwards
and can't go backwards

Hitting the baseball
over the fence brings scouts to
scribble down my name

Chasing high fly balls
just for the sheer joy of it
is an inner test

Sometimes when the ball
leaves your hand you know it is
good without looking

Writing down the poem
is like releasing the animal
after you have captured it

Write as if you're dead
I once heard this said
not an easy task

Publishing a poem
does not matter in the end
the joy was telling

I have done my best
to write from my heart and mind
I bid you adieu

Afterthought

To accept who we are and say it's OK

To believe or not believe what we were told when we
were children

To believe or not believe what the world has told us
about ourselves

To see through the illusions and fog
and trust on what true merit to evaluate one's self

Is this not a lifelong struggle?

The author was born in Paterson, New Jersey and moved to Brooklyn, New York around age 4 Graduated from Richmond College City University of New York with a degree in Psychology and received a Masters in Counseling from Long Island University. Member of the Bonnies Boys Club Baseball Hall of Fame. For the last twenty years he has resided with his wife and son in Montclair and Cedar Grove, New Jersey.

Made in the USA
Columbia, SC
01 September 2017